Goddesses

Susan Seddon Boulet • Coloring book

Many ancient cultures around the world have told stories and made drawings, paintings, or sculptures about goddesses. These female gods were thought to have great powers for protection, nurturing, beauty, healing, and hunting. Many goddesses were depicted in both human and animal forms. Bast, the Egyptian goddess, is represented as a cat. Eagle Woman is a bird goddess who symbolizes spirit, valor, majesty, renewal, and keen vision.

Artist Susan Seddon Boulet interpreted many different goddesses in her dreamlike paintings. This coloring book includes Aphrodite, Greek goddess of love and beauty; Padma with her lotus flower, Hindu goddess of wealth, abundance, and beauty; and Hera, Greek goddess of the heavens, the earth, the seas, and the underworld.

The twenty-two paintings shown on the insides of this coloring book's covers show strong and powerful goddesses. Susan Seddon Boulet's paintings use many different colors and symbols. Look closely! You can use these vibrant images to guide you as you color in the pages just like the artist, or to help inspire your own unique color and pattern combinations. We've even left one blank page at the back so that you can imagine a goddess of your own. Don't forget to include symbols of her mysterious powers.

Pomegranate

All artworks are by Susan Seddon Boulet (American, b. Brazil, 1941–1997).

1. *Etain*, 1995
2. *Guinevere*, n.d.
3. *Skywatcher*, 1972
4. *Triple Goddess*, 1987
5. *Aditi*, 1973
6. *Dhisana*, 1979
7. *Eve*, n.d.
8. *Diana*, 1972
9. *Hera*, 1975
10. *Padma*, 1976
11. *Amphitrite*, 1975
12. *Bast*, 1981
13. *Isis*, 1978
14. *Fati*, n.d.
15. *Kuan Yin*, 1985
16. *Sedna*, 1977
17. *Aphrodite*, 1979
18. *Hel*, n.d.
19. *Sekhmet*, 1981
20. *Flidais*, 1977
21. *Selene*, 1979
22. *Eagle Woman*, 1986

Pomegranate Communications, Inc.
19018 NE Portal Way, Portland OR 97230
800 227 1428 www.pomegranate.com

Color reproductions © 2014 E. Boulet
Line drawings © Pomegranate Communications, Inc.

Item No. CB162
Designed by Carey Hall. Line drawings by Becky Holtzman.

Printed in Korea

25 24 23 22 21 20 19 18 17 16   11 10 9 8 7 6 5 4 3 2

Distributed by Pomegranate Europe Ltd.
Unit 1, Heathcote Business Centre, Hurlbutt Road
Warwick, Warwickshire CV34 6TD, UK
[+44] 0 1926 430111
sales@pomeurope.co.uk

1. *Etain*

2. Guinevere

3. Skywatcher

4. *Triple Goddess*

5. *Aditi*

6. *Dhisana*

7. Eve

8. *Diana*

9. *Hera*

10. *Padma*

11. *Amphitrite*

12. Bast

13. *Isis*

14. *Fati*

15. *Kuan Yin*

16. *Sedna*

17. *Aphrodite*

18. *Hel*

19. Sekhmet

20. *Flidais*

21. *Selene*

22. Eagle Woman

Draw and color your own picture here!